What People Are Saying About
Coping with Physical Loss ar

"This workbook is very good stimuli for focusing on issues that are cru~   ~h loss and disability. Just putting the questions with the blanks together is a great opportun~~   ~ lection and might greatly help people raise their consciousness. As I believe the saying goes 'If you do not help yourself, then no one will be able to help you.'"
—Beni R. Jakob, Ph.D, Israeli Arthritis Foundation (INBAR)

"Ritter provides a valuable self-care plan for those suffering from the loss of physical capacity. He also shows readers how to find the mental, emotional and spiritual encouragement critical to the healing process."
—Georgiann Baldino, Author and cancer support-group facilitator

"People—even mental health professionals—erroneously assume that grief is a reaction limited to the loss of a loved one. But grieving is a far more universal response. Losing one's bodily integrity or functioning ('physical loss') provokes mourning and a distorted self-image. The horror and recoil that disabilities elicit in the healthy only compound the victim's sense of deprivation and worthlessness.

This book is a set of guided questions intended to assist the afflicted to heal from such traumas. Based on experience with 100 patients, it is straightforward and structured. The progression is logical and transparent. The patient or client is coaxed into facing his or her condition and predicament squarely and honestly and into recruiting all resources—including his family, friends, and social milieu—to fight depression, rage, and helplessness.

Though slender, the workbook is indispensable to victims of physical loss, their nearest and dearest, medical staff, and psychotherapists or grief counselors."
—Sam Vaknin, Ph.D., author of *Malignant Self Love: Narcissism Revisited*

"Rick Ritter captures the depth of the emotional pain in the aftermath of physical loss and disability. This workbook format will surely provide a sense empowerment to those who feel helpless in these situations."
—Rev. James W. Clifton, Ph.D., LCSW

"I found the workbook useful in addressing the various aspects of the physical loss. The examples given by the author are very relevant and will help the sufferer relate to similar situations. I recommend the workbook to those who are trying to heal from past traumas or to those who are trying to help their near and dear heal."
— S.V. Swamy, Holistic Healer and editor of *Homeopathy For Everyone*

"This workbook is more than just a set of exercises, valuable as that can be. It is an inspiration, a guide, and in some cases may become a lifesaver. The author himself has suffered severe physical problems and has surmounted them. So he is not some 'expert' telling you what to do, but rather a guide who has been there himself. A lot of my work deals with chronic pain management and this workbook will be invaluable to my clients."
—Robert Rich, Ph.D., author of "Cancer: A Personal Challenge"

"This workbook is a tremendous resource that is practical and easy to use. The author shows his connection with this material in a way from which we can all benefit."
—Geneva Reynaga-Abiko, Psy.D., Clinical Psychologist
University of Illinois, Urbana-Champaign Counseling Center

"This workbook helps people understand the grieving that occurs with physical loss and helps readers cope with their decreases in functioning. Additionally, the book asks people to search for positives that have happened, rather than dwelling totally in the negative."
—Susan Yost, LISW

"As a person with an acquired disability and a social worker who has experience working with persons who have either acquired or congenital disabilities I see the usefulness and importance *of Coping with Physical Loss and Disability: A Workbook*. To date I have not seen another tool that can help people who have disabilities become self-aware and adjust to their new lives. This Workbook can help them to see how they still have strengths and abilities and move beyond being disabled to reestablish their self-acceptance and functionality.

"If it had been written two decades earlier, this tool would have been very helpful to me after my motorcycle accident when I was 16. It would have helped me, and many of the clients with disabilities I have worked with over the years, to focus on what I had left instead of wallowing on what I had lost. I will be using this workbook with clients in the future and strongly recommend its use to any person who is working with persons with disabilities."
—Ian Landry, MSW, RSW

"Rick Ritter is able to provide us with an insightful road map to the growth process of individuals experiencing physical loss. As clinicians we often need to provide support to those who have experienced much more loss than we ever can imagine. This workbook is a masterpiece in helping us accomplish that proficiency."
—Darlene DiGorio-Hevner, LCSW

---

*"To be what we are,
and to become what we are capable of becoming,
is the only end in life"*
—Robert Louis Stevenson (June 1880)

Loving Healing Press is dedicated to producing books about innovative and rapid therapies which redefine what is possible for healing the mind and spirit.

Coping With Physical Loss and Disability:

A Workbook

By Rick Ritter, MSW

Additional Illustrations by Tyler Mills

New Horizons in Therapy Series

Coping with Physical Loss and Disability: A Workbook

First Edition: January 2006

ISBN-10: 1-932690-18-2

Library of Congress Cataloging-in-Publication Data

Ritter, Rick, 1948-
  Coping with physical loss and disability : a workbook / by Rick Ritter.-- 1st ed.
    p. cm. -- (New horizons in therapy series)
  Includes bibliographical references and index.
  ISBN-13: 978-1-932690-18-7 (pbk. : alk. paper)
  ISBN-10: 1-932690-18-2 (pbk. : alk. paper)
 1. Grief therapy--Handbooks, manuals, etc. 2. People with disabilities--Mental health--Handbooks, manuals, etc. 3. People with disabilities--Psychology--Handbooks, manuals, etc. 4. Loss (Psychology)--Handbooks, manuals, etc. I. Title. II. Series.
RC455.4.L67R58 2006
362.4--dc22
                          2005024924

Distributed by:
Baker & Taylor, Ingram Book Group, New Leaf Distributing

Published by:
Loving Healing Press
5145 Pontiac Trail
Ann Arbor, MI 48105
USA

http://www.LovingHealing.com or
info@LovingHealing.com
Fax +1 734 663 6861

"So many of our dreams at first seem impossible, then they seem improbable, and then, when we summon the will, they soon become inevitable."

—Christopher Reeve, August 26th, 1996

(Actor, Director, Philanthropist, also a quadriplegic)

- **Got parts? An Insider's Guide to Managing Life Successfully with Dissociative Identity Disorder, by ATW**

- **Coping with Physical Loss and Disability: A Workbook, by Rick Ritter, MSW**

About our Series Editor, Robert Rich, Ph.D.

Loving Healing Press is pleased to announce Robert Rich, Ph.D. as Series Editor for the *New Horizons in Therapy Series*. This exciting new series plans to bring you the best of person-centered therapies in practical application, theory, and self-help formats.

Robert Rich, M.Sc., Ph.D., M.A.P.S., A.A.S.H. is a highly experienced counseling psychologist. His web site www.anxietyanddepression-help.com is a storehouse of helpful information for people suffering from anxiety and depression.

Bob is also a multiple award-winning writer of both fiction and non-fiction, and a professional editor. His writing is displayed at www.bobswriting.com. You are advised not to visit him there unless you have the time to get lost for a while.

Three of his books are tools for psychological self-help: *Anger and Anxiety: Be in charge of your emotions and control phobias*, *Personally Speaking: Single session email therapy*, and *Cancer: A personal challenge*. However, his philosophy and psychological knowledge come through in all his writing, which is perhaps why three of his books have won international awards, and he has won many minor prizes. Dr. Rich currently resides at Wombat Hollow in Australia.

About the Cover

The cover image depicts an adult female as read by a 3-D scanner and then rendered as a polygonized surface by Imageware 12. A red-marble bottom texture on the body indicates fissures and loss in the body. A transparent-steel top texture on the body, which mostly shows as reflection, represents resilience of the spirit. Blue sky and fair weather clouds represent the possibility of hope and healing.

Special thanks go to www.BigFoto.com, the royalty-free photo agency offering free use of all pictures (with link or reference), for use of the sky background picture.

Creative director for the cover was Victor R. Volkman.

Table of Contents

Table of Figures

Preface

I developed the questions in this workbook with help from a variety of sources. I must give credit to Enid Traisman, MSW, who has authored several grief journals and it was my utilization of her journals with my clients over time that got me thinking about the issue of physical loss. On several occasions, I modified her journals and edited the text of a grief journal in order to fit the needs of a client with physical loss issues. By osmosis, I benefited from this process myself, given that I was undergoing the last two of thirteen knee operations and my physical capacities were changing again. Additionally, I had been diagnosed with asthma, which impacted my physical capacities as well. The questions themselves went through a process of transformation as clients asked what this meant or what that meant and the clarification process proceeded over a matter of several years.

I was initially discouraged that I could find no such resource for physical loss issues at the time I began working on this project. However, I was ultimately encouraged that I could develop something to assist in the healing process of persons with any type of physical loss. Many types of physical losses are of the disenfranchised variety in that they are invisible to others or they are thought to be simply a matter of aging. Of course, this invisibility phenomenon appears in many other types of loss as well.

There are many facets to physical loss, but let's just take a quick look at two critical issues: the age of onset and the manner in which the loss occurs. For example, the struggle that young people face when they have a pacemaker installed at age fifteen or a heart transplant at sixteen is beyond the imagination of most of us. The manner in which it occurs, whether debilitating disease or sudden trauma, directly impacts the way in which I personally perceive my own loss and the way others perceive it, whether they be family, friends or neighbors.

I have used this workbook with more than a hundred clients over a ten year period and I have shared it with other therapists around the country. I have even mailed it to other persons working toward recovery who have heard about it and requested a copy for their own. I am therefore pleased to present this edition through Loving Healing Press in hopes of reaching out to more people in search of recovery. I would also like to acknowledge Tyler Mills for providing much of the artwork to this volume.

—Rick Ritter, MSW

What is Physical Loss?

Physical loss is a result of having suffered physical harm or injury—it is a reduction in one's personal capacity to do or be. This can happen gradually in a declining manner or it can happen instantly as in a traumatic accident. Physical loss means that the original physical capacity has been destroyed beyond repair. Of course, there are various degrees of physical loss:

- Partial loss of function—capacity is partially reduced or destroyed
- Total loss of function—severe near total incapacitation physically
- Damaged self-image—being deprived of what one once had

Physical loss implies that there is a grief or mourning process that is either underway or that it is frozen and not moving forward.

A partial list of losses might include the following aspects:

- Sensory: hearing, vision, touch, etc.

- Direct physical results of traumatic injury: scars, burns, paralysis, amputation, speech deficits, stroke, progressive diseases.

- Disease: either directly due to the disease or to the treatment process: HIV, cancer, diabetes, hepatitis, muscular dystrophy, multiple sclerosis, and lupus just to name a few.

- Surgical treatment effects: mastectomies, colostomies, radiation, chemotherapy, orthopedic implants, amputation, reproductive failure, and hair loss.

- Indirect physical results: muscle wasting, onset of obesity, and loss of energy, mobility, and independence.

The above losses come about as a result of some of these: diabetes, cancer, traumatic injury, neuromuscular disease, lupus, skin diseases, burns, aging, surgeries, strokes, heart attacks, and abuse or neglect.

Loss has a far reaching impact on people and their surroundings. Unfortunately many of the views and attitudes regarding physical loss lead us down the path to a disenfranchised treatment of the loss itself. If a person has physically recovered or healed as much as he/she can or will, then we assume healing is over and nothing else needs to be done. In fact, the healing is just beginning, but without the proper ingredients for the continued healing of the person emotionally, psychologically, and spiritually, it too gets amputated.

Along with the physical loss, there is a loss of dreams and expectations for one's life. As long as these non-physical losses go unhealed, the consequences to a person and his/her world are incalculable. It is also critical for the physical loss to be dealt with in a holistic manner. If not, the person is likely to suffer emotionally and enter into a state of chronic stress. This in turn will lead to further physical losses, and handicap the immune system as well.

Getting Started

It is quite surreal to review the landscape of our lives sometimes, taking into account the incidents that caused our physical loss and subsequent surgeries, treatments, rehabilitation. Meanwhile, we live out daily the results (temporary and permanent) of the variety of physical losses that we have endured. The work that has culminated in the writing of this guided workbook will assist and support you in achieving the most complete recovery from whatever losses you may be enduring. It makes no difference what the loss is or whether others see it as a loss, it has still changed your life and the lives of others.

Be assured that there is something you can do to come to terms with your loss. It is in our best interests to recover from these losses as completely as we can, so that we may live our lives at the highest possible level of functioning and quality. Not one of us can afford to store the emotional materials from physical losses, especially in light of the craziness that swirls around us all every day on this planet. Choosing recovery and resilience allows us to exist and carry on.

Before reading this workbook, select at least three significant persons in your life whom you can choose to share this work with as you follow the path to recovery. You may choose more than three, but at least select this many as a part of your commitment to healing yourself.

Although this workbook is designed for you to write in as you explore your personal path, you need not limit yourself to the pages provided herein. You may want to have a loose-leaf binder or journal for recording observations or insights that go beyond what can fit in a box.

1 Past and Future

Many frustrations and misunderstandings arise from intermixing the past and the future. In this chapter, you will look at your beliefs in both areas.

A person can best be described by considering four aspects: emotional, mental, physical and spiritual. All four are important, and they interact in complex ways. You have undergone some distressing physical losses. The impact of these on your life will depend on the emotions you feel about them, your thoughts, and the way you conceive of your place in the universe.

Steve was born with no apparent disabilities, but as a young boy was diagnosed with muscular dystrophy and by age 11 or so he was in a wheelchair. Steve almost grew up with his disabilities since he was diagnosed at such a young age. However, he eventually lost all of his peers whom he had met and become friends with through his Muscular Dystrophy Association (MDA) contacts, because he outlived all of them by quite a few years. He finally died at the age of 29 from complications of MD and from complications of HIV. He had contracted HIV via a blood transfusion during a surgery to place rods in his back. Steve lived a relatively happy life within his limits. in spite of the double-whammy dealt to him by life.

Mike was an angry young man whom I worked with at the request of his wife and medical support staff due to his anger and his subsequent lashing out at all of them. He had been wrestling with a friend in his backyard in his mid-twenties and his friend broke Mike's neck. He became a quadriplegic[1] ("quad") instantly and he had gone from being a roofer to an angry trapped young man relegated to his hospital bed and medical equipment and having to rely on others for his every need. His daughter, who was five, had really gotten to him when she defied his verbal correction and instruction and mocked him, saying, "I don't have to listen to you anymore—you can't catch me." Initially he didn't respond very well, but eventually he moderated his response and worked within his limits to improve his response to others on most days.

Larry had become a quad when he and a buddy were driving while drunk. His buddy died and he was left a quadriplegic. He had gone from working in his own business and riding and caring for horses and motocross bikes to being confined to bed and then eventually to an electric wheelchair since his fracture had been a high one. He terrorized his family either from bed or from the chair. I witnessed him pinning his daughter against the wall with the wheelchair when she was in her teens. He still clung to the idea that he was the king of his roost and he used any means to control others about him. Yet when he was in a public setting, he often would be confronted with the looks and the questions from children and he would break down crying. However, he quickly he switched back to anger as his preferred mode of expression. No one ever reached him and he never worked beyond the anger and the guilt of his situation. He died fairly isolated and most people wanted nothing to do with him.

Mike came to terms with his anger while Larry let it run rampant and destroy both himself and his family relationships.

---

[1] Quadriplegia is caused by damage to the spinal cord at a high level (e.g. cervical spine) or the brain. The injury causes the victim to lose either total or partial use of the arms and legs. The condition is also termed tetraplegia; both terms mean "paralysis of four limbs". There are about 5,000 cervical spinal cord injuries per year in America, and about 1,000 per year in the UK. In some rare cases, through intensive rehabilitation, slight movement can be regained (source: Wikipedia)

These four aspects of a human being (emotional, mental, physical and spiritual) are important in every one of the exercises in this workbook.

1-1. Who are you today? This question requires that you describe who you are in written words, drawings, collages, paintings, clay work, movement or any other expressive means that you are comfortable with or have the ability to accomplish. Select at least two methods of answering this question. Creative activities will reveal a great deal of useful information to you. Art therapy is based on the belief that the creative process involved in the making of art is healing and life-enhancing[2]. **Take into account in this question, and all the rest of the questions in this workbook that the "you" we are referring to is the emotional, mental, physical and spiritual you. Consider all four of these aspects of yourself in each set of answers.**

---

[2] For more information about Art Therapy, please visit the American Art Therapy Association at http://www.arttherapy.org/

1-2. Who do you see yourself as having been prior to this current loss?

Use the same techniques as for the first exercise. However, don't just remember. Before starting to do the work, close your eyes, breathe quietly and 'go back' to the way things were then.

1-3. Who can you become? Some people find it difficult to answer this question. If this is the case for you, ask others who know you fairly well. This will give you a start. (You may also return to this and other questions and answer them in more complete ways as you progress through this workbook.)

1-4. What are your abilities currently? This would include physical activities, work and relationships with people.

1-5. What limitations do you currently have? This would include physical, emotional, mental and spiritual areas of your life.

1-6. Of the two previous questions, which one required more thought and effort in answering, and why?

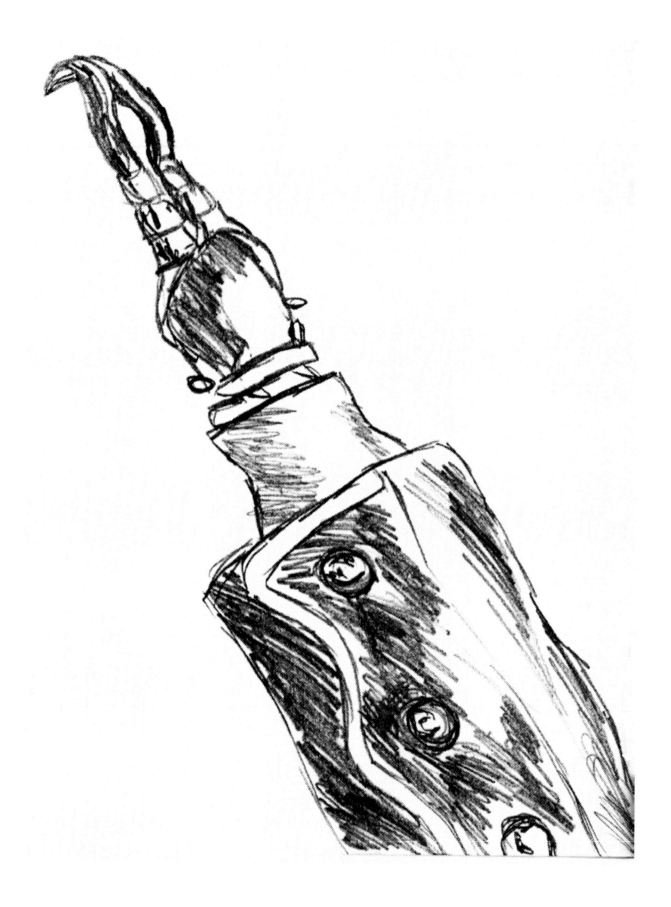

2 | Self-Care and Support

Self-care and your support system are two of the biggest contributing factors to your ongoing success and quality of life. In this chapter, we'll begin by looking at what's available with and without these factors.

Pam, when she was younger (20-30), had been burning off her garden at the end of the season and she caught herself on fire with the help of a gusty wind. She suffered 3rd degree burns over 40% of her body and wore a burn bodysuit for over a year. Even though it seemed like an insurmountable situation, she continued to be an effective mom to three kids, to keep her job, and to prosper. Pam had a good support system of family and friends. She survived to be a good mom, good employee and learned so many lessons regarding life that she remains a resilient person today.

Juanita has a form of Multiple Sclerosis[1] and is confined to her bed at home. Her husband divorced her once she was correctly diagnosed (which took several years) and he has consistently kept their 10 year old son away from her. She is bedridden and lives by herself. As her physical capacity diminished, friends and family have slowly dropped out of her life to the point that she is angry and isolated. Most folks won't trouble to check in on her and they almost never bother to take her out anywhere in the community because it is difficult. Her support before and as a result of MS presently is almost nonexistent and her quality of life suffers from that.

Bob returned from Viet Nam a shattered person physically and emotionally. There isn't room here to share the whole story, but as an amputee he had immediate support at home from his father because his own father had lost a leg in World War II. Sometimes the support we have doesn't match up with the continued losses that occur. For example, Bob's son died later in a gravel pit cave-in and his daughter is today dying of MS. He is helpless today while he watches her slowly die and his old wounds continue to be torn open emotionally. Sometimes it is difficult to find enough support for all that happens in life. Fortunately, Bob utilized the local Vet Center program for individual and group therapy and it was very much like a second family for him.

While moving furniture, Jim tore the ligaments in his knee. The doctor arranged surgery, but since this was an 'elective procedure', there was a waiting list of six months. He had a casual job as a waiter, and so he lost his source of income. Why was he moving furniture? Because his fiancée left him, and took up with another guy. He was new in the area and had few friends or even acquaintances. He didn't have a car—until then, Brenda had driven him around, but now she was gone.

The result was complete, suicidal depression for Jim. He didn't get out of bed in the morning. He ate very little, and couldn't get his act together enough to access available support resources. He was at risk of being evicted from his house.

This tragedy was the result, not so much of the original injury, but of his lack of social support. Contrast his story with that of Peter, a young man who was badly handicapped in a motorcycle accident. His

---

[1] Multiple sclerosis (MS) is a degenerative disorder of the central nervous system thought to have an autoimmune mechanism. It can present with a variety of neurological symptoms occurring in attacks, or slowly progressing over time. It has no cure yet and the exact cause remains unknown. Due to its effects of the nervous system, it can lead to long-term impaired mobility and disability in more severe cases. (source: Wikipedia)

injuries were far worse than Jim's, and included permanent loss of function in one arm and one leg. He certainly didn't enjoy the pain, but coped incredibly well, and achieved remarkable healing months faster than the medical prediction.

Why? He has a loving partner, is the father of a little child and is surrounded by friends who care about him. He is a musician, loves to garden, carves little statues from wood and manages to have a sense of humor even when in pain. These inner and environmental resources gave Peter the strength to conquer the worst effects of his injuries.

Fortunately, Jim contacted a psychologist, who talked him through the worst of his depression. Once he got started, he obtained financial assistance, and soon a support network of community agencies filling the vacuum of his personal social situation. He still hobbles around painfully, but now has hope, knows there is a future, and can cope.

These real stories emphasize the need for drawing on your inner resources, and on the support of other people. The following exercises help you to map these. Take your time in listing the answers to each question. You may find some answers that surprise you, and lead you to previously unrecognized resources.

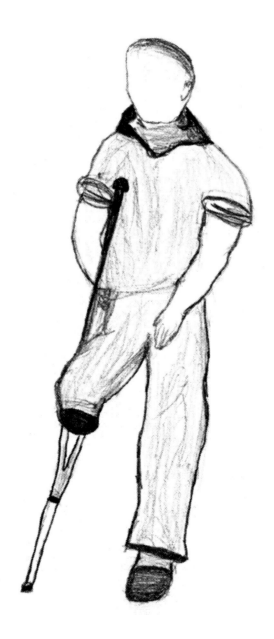

2-1. What support systems do you currently have in your life? This includes family, friends, co-workers, neighbors, medical staff, etc.

2-2. How can you expand your personal support system and what would make it more effective? Where might you find help that you can access without feeling that you are a load on others? Remember, there are agencies and voluntary organizations in many places that help people who need it.

2-3. What things do you do, or have you done in the past to take care of yourself? Again, take into account the mental, emotional, physical and spiritual parts of your life. This includes nutrition, exercise and other ways of caring for your physical health, activities to stimulate your mind, creative pursuits, enjoyment of beauty such as gardening or being in nature, activities that make you laugh, those that are of service to others (the more you give the more you get), and times when you still your mind such as prayer or meditation.

Develop a self-care plan by which you can take better care of yourself and make progress in becoming more resilient.

PART 1—SELF-CARE PROCESS

We must know our needs in order to develop a self-care plan that has a chance to positively impact in our life. Consider your answers to previous questions to determine where you need to make changes in your mental, emotional, spiritual and physical situation.

2-4-1. List your needs:

2-4-2. How could your needs be met?

2-4-3. What are you committing yourself to doing?

2-4-4. What will you ask others to assist you in accomplishing?

PART 2—SCHEDULING

Next, we'll look at how you are approaching the demands of your life, given your resources, looking for a well-balanced plan of action. For example, if it is all slanted toward work, we have a life out of balance. The kinds of things that should go in your weekly schedule should reflect a balanced approach to living and coping with whatever you are facing each week: school, work, childcare, physical therapy, church, exercise, and recreational activity. You also need to take into account the limits of the people providing you with care and support when formulating this plan.

- Review and revise the schedule and the self-care plan every few months or if there are significant changes in your life or limitations that throw the whole thing out of balance again.

- If it is not a fairly smooth operating plan, or if it becomes difficult to implement, then you need to review the schedule and the plan to achieve a more balanced approach.

- It is very beneficial to have others review the schedule and the plan in order to obtain as objective a view point as possible, and a plan that has the maximum possibility for success.

SAMPLE SCHEDULE

My Weekly Schedule is:

Monday
8-9:30am PT at the rehab center
10-noon study time
1-3pm vocational class at the comm. college

Tuesday
9-5pm work
7-9pm basketball practice

Wednesday
10-11am weekly session with Bob
1-3pm vocational class at the comm. college
4-5:30pm PT at the rehab center

My Weekly Schedule is:

Monday

Tuesday

Wednesday

Thursday

Friday

Saturday

Sunday

My schedule for re-evaluation of this plan is _____.

PART 3—SELF-CARE STRATEGIES

Your complete self-care plan will address the mental, emotional, physical, and spiritual aspects of your life. In this exercise, you'll invent fifteen self-care strategies, without any duplications, in each of the four aspects. Self-care strategy is anything that makes one feel better about themselves and doesn't infringe on others or create an unsafe situation for anyone. This probably seems quite abstract right now, so let's look quickly at some examples. **There are no wrong categories to place items of self care in for this exercise as long as they don't harm you or anyone else.** For example, massage might mean either emotional, physical, or spiritual care to you.

SAMPLE SELF-CARE PLAN

MENTAL	EMOTIONAL	PHYSICAL	SPIRITUAL
Jigsaw puzzles[2]	Talk with a friend or family member that I trust.	Lift weights.	Pray.
Gardening.	Tai Chi	Ride bike (stationary or handcycle[3]).	Spending time in church or with others who enrich my life.
Journaling.	Massage.	Walk.	Study in whatever words enrich my life.
Flying a kite.	Time with children, grandchildren, or just children down the block.	Spend any kind of time in nature (rain or shine or flurries).	Meditation
Reading.	Listen to music	Progressive muscle relaxation.	Yoga.
Watch a movie or listen to books on tape.	Visualize places I have been and things I have done, even if I was able bodied at that time.	Isometric exercises.	Art (drawing, painting, sculpture, ...)
Therapeutic techniques (see Appendix A).	Feeding birds and squirrels.	Taking care of a pet.	Singing or chanting

---

[2] Especially so it can be left out for extended periods of time.

[3] For information on hand-powered cycling products, see www.FreedomRyder.com.

My Self-Care Plan

MENTAL	EMOTIONAL	PHYSICAL	SPIRITUAL

2-5. What areas of your life have been affected by this loss? List each area of your life that has been affected by this loss and in what ways that area of your life has been affected. Again, take your time over this one. You might resort to some of the techniques described in question 1-1 to explore your hidden losses. By identifying your needs, you can take steps to improve your situation.

2-6. Fill out the eco-map that on p. 25, outlining the people in your life who are a support for you or the people in your life who are a strain on your ability to recover. You may want to look at the sample eco-map to understand how relationships are mapped.

ECO-MAP

Fill in connections where they exist. Indicate nature of strong connections with a descriptive word or by drawing lines ———— for strong - - - - - for weak ++++ for stressful
Draw arrows along lines to signify the flow of energy, resources, etc.
Identify significant people and fill in circles as needed.

ECO-MAP

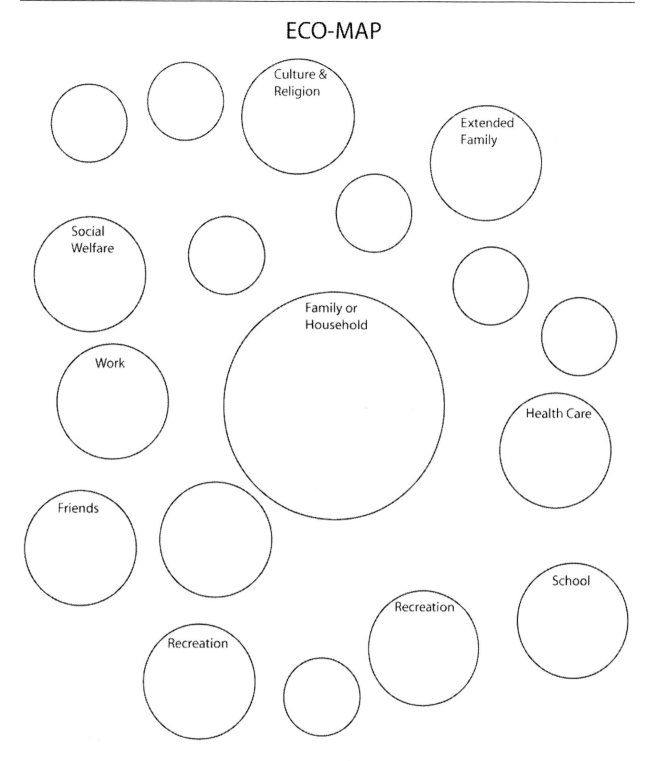

Fill in connections where they exist. Indicate nature of strong connections with a descriptive word or by
drawing lines ———— for strong - - - - - for weak ++++ for stressful
Draw arrows along lines to signify the flow of energy, resources, etc.
Identify significant people and fill in circles as needed.

3 Dealing with Loss: Feelings and Beliefs

"I have to challenge myself constantly not to lose my vision about what I can become. I have to remind myself constantly that life is a daring adventure—or nothing!"
—Max Cleland in *Going for the Max! 12 Principles for Living Life to the Fullest* (2000)

Max Cleland suffered severe wounds after less than a year of his volunteer tour of duty in Viet Nam and returned from the war as a triple-amputee. While recuperating from his injuries, he was elected to the Georgia State Senate. In 1975, when he was 34 years old, President Carter appointed him administrator of the Veteran's Administration, where he instituted the revolutionary "Vets Center program," which for the first time offered psychological counseling as well as physical care to combat veterans. He later served in the US Senate as chairman of an Armed Services Committee. Though people often disagree with his political views, his voice is always heard. You can read his autobiography in *Strong at the Broken Places* (2000).

"Here's the moment: after he got out of the pool, looking like a statue of a Greek god ravaged by time, Xavier Torres slipped on a pair of artificial legs and strode away, in every sense, six feet tall."
—Marlowe Hood on the defining moment of the 2004 Athens Paralympic Games.

Torres is missing both hands and his right forearm, and both his legs have been amputated above the knee. He was born with a congenital amputation[1]. "I am the only one in my family who was born handicapped, and I've been happy with myself since the beginning. I don't know what I would say or how it would be like in normal conditions. I am conscious of my handicap. I am not like almost everyone else, but handicapped people have a bigger adaptation capacity. That's why my handicap is not important for me."

Torres holds the paralympic world record for endurance swimming: 58km (35 miles) in 24 hours. He has beaten a total of 26 world records since 1991. He's also a TV sports commentator in Spain.

"I've always loved sports. Since I was a child, I used to play with a ball or a racket every minute because it made me happy. When I wake up in the morning, the last thing that I think about, if I do, is that I have to wear those artificial legs for me to walk. When I was back in school, I never felt different, I used to feel as normal as the rest of the people in my class," remembers Xavier. "I began to swim almost like a therapy, in the water I used to feel better, to feel free, with more movement and coordination. At the beginning I had a trainer called Lorenzo who taught me a lot of things and María Castañer, my second trainer, took me to the world of competition." You can learn more about him at www.XaviTorres.com.

"When I see him 'flying' in the water, it's as if God himself is there with him, giving Xavi all the power, it's just like as if all the people in the world could be reflected in his vitality."   — Olympic gold medalist Kevin Berry on Xavier Torres

---

[1] Congenital amputation is the absence of a fetal limb or fetal part at birth. This condition may be the result of the constriction of fibrous bands within the membrane that surrounds the developing fetus (amniotic band syndrome) or the exposure to substances known to cause birth defects (teratogenic agents) such as Thalidomide. Other factors, including genetics, may also play a role. (Source: Joseph F. Smith Medical Library).

3-1. Think back to before your current loss situation, and list a few losses you'd endured during the preceding year or so. These can be major or minor, covering all kinds of situations. You can also list losses suffered by people you know well, and even characters from TV shows, books and movies. Organize these events along the timeline on p.31.

3-2. How did you (or the other person who suffered the loss) deal with the situation? For each instance you listed, think about and set out what made it possible to first accept the loss, then to live with it, and finally to get over it? You are now finding resources you may be able to apply to your present situation.

But don't stop here. There is still a bounty of resources to be explored. Now repeat exercises 3-1 and 3-2 for times further back, eventually right back to your childhood.

Events - Timeline

The tick marks above might represent "Years and Months" or "Months and Weeks" since your physical loss started. Be sure to note all injuries, major medical interventions, and loss or recovery of abilities over time.

3-3. How have you dealt with your major physical loss up to the present? Think of daily events and encounters you have had with people and describe how you have managed this loss so far. You are currently coming to terms with a loss. To improve your ability to reach a satisfactory adaptation to your new situation, whether it is temporary or permanent, you will find it useful to explore how you surmounted past difficulties. You have, within you and within your circle of supports, many resources for doing so, but when you are distressed, it is easy to lose sight of the positives and focus in on the negative. Therefore, the next few exercises will explore the way you have coped with previous losses within your experience. In this context, it will be useful to examine how you handled losses of all kinds, not just deaths, but for example also loss of contact with a person you liked, loss of a job, lost opportunities, hopes that were not realized... It will also be useful to remember how other people you know well have handled their losses. By thinking about this, you may learn from them.

How I have dealt with my major physical loss is:

3-4. How can you change and improve the manner in which you are currently dealing with the loss? This is now applying the resources you have uncovered. You will find that, having explored your past successes in handling losses, your beliefs about your current situation will have changed. You now have the power to improve what is important: your feelings.

So, next we need to explore your particular, unique way of handling feelings. There is no general prescription for everyone, therefore the following exercises will enable you to construct a method to suit you.

3-5-1. What feelings are you comfortable expressing in private, as in keeping to yourself?
Often I have encountered people who are uncomfortable letting their feelings out even in total privacy. This wouldn't be so problematic except that for many people who don't find an avenue for venting their feelings it leads to physical and emotional difficulties which hinder our ability to succeed in relationships and ultimately in life. Answering this question will allow you to gauge for yourself your ability to operate emotionally and see clearly if you have obstacles that are in your path in life.

3-5-2. What feelings are you comfortable expressing to people you completely trust?

3-5-3. What are your beliefs about expressing those feelings? As you think on this question reflect back over recent times and list the times and/or events that have brought about in you a level of discomfort that you have noticed in your mind. Attempt to recreate these situations by writing them down and notice what you feel and what you tell yourself internally to resolve or take care of those problematic moments. I would also suggest that you select one or two people you trust and ask them for feedback about how they view your style of dealing with feelings—whatever they have to say may be enlightening in a variety of ways. It is also important to write, in as much detail as possible, what you consider your normal or natural or usual way of dealing with your feelings.

Some examples of styles of emotional expression are:

avoidant	equal	controlling
spontaneous	neutral	conflicted
passive	direct	superior
empathetic	defensive	distanced
listener	non-feeling	rigid

...just to name a few.

3-7. What feelings are the most difficult for you to deal with currently, and why?

3-8. What feelings do you currently consider to be unacceptable, and why? It's OK to have whatever thoughts, feelings and emotions arise. However, we don't need to accept them, or to act on them.

3-9. What are your feelings and beliefs about loss, and how does that affect you as an individual?

3-10. How much affect does your loss affect your gender role (male or female)? This may involve aspects such as body image, sexuality and competence to do tasks you consider to be within your capabilities. Also consider what you think people expect of you because you are male or female and in this circumstance.

Having done this analysis, you will be fully aware of your feelings as they are now. This means that where you are satisfied with them, you can be pleased with yourself; where you are dissatisfied, you can start on the work of changing them.

Other essential factors of your loss are age (stage in life), financial obligations and responsibilities, and long term plans and hopes.

4 | Understanding Disability

Disability means different things to different people. In this chapter, you will look at your core beliefs about disability and how it affects your world-view. You will also confront how others view disability and how it affects their view of you.

Georgia Gilbert was the first disabled person I remember encountering in life. She was a 40-year-old fiery single-leg amputee. I have rarely seen someone who was so fluid with her disability in life. She was most adept at using just one crutch—to my young amazement. Georgia was one of the smiling-est people I can recall from my childhood. She was rarely discouraged and consistently upbeat as a result of her supportive family and her steadfast religious beliefs. She was a fixture in the church community I grew up in. Georgia left an indelible mark on my mind and contributed, at least in part, to how I have been able to cope over the years.

Linda, my office manager when I worked at the Vet Center, was an example of resiliency in the face of disability. She began as a part of our team in 1980 when we launched our local outreach center and opened the program. She had already been diagnosed with Multiple Sclerosis, but still walked rather well with a cane. As time went along her balance deteriorated and so did her muscle tone, and with it, her capacity to do physical things slowly diminished. When I left that program in late 1987, Linda had become wheelchair-bound, but she still continued to work and be a part of the healing in the lives of thousand of vets and their families. She may have indeed shortened her life a bit by enduring a very stressful job. Ultimately she was unable to continue ambulating and became bedridden and ultimately ended up in a nursing home for the last few years of her life. Her remarkable resiliency derived from doing something she truly loved to do and from the total support from her loving husband Randy, who stayed with her to the very end. She died several years ago, but she has not been forgotten nor has this diminished the contribution she made in the lives of many.

4-1-1. Describe your thoughts on receiving help from other people. When is it okay and when is it not okay to receive that help from others? Focus on your feelings. You can do this, again, through the creative activities described in 1-1, or by closing your eyes, and actually 'going back' to a recent occasion when someone offered to help you, or you needed to ask help from another person.

4-1-2. When you are helped by someone what is your response and why? (examples are: gratitude, shame, guilt, resentment, anger, indebtedness)

4-1-3. When you are unable to obtain assistance from anyone what is your response and why? (examples are: anger, relief, sadness, frustration, hurt, resentment, jealousy)

4-2. How does your current loss limit you? Consider the previous usual activities of your life: school or work; personal care like dressing, hygiene, eating; mobility including driving a car if that was a part of your repertoire; sport, hobbies and entertainment, etc.

4-3. How many disabled persons do you know? Remember that "disabled" includes a wide variety of losses, for example intellectual limitations, diabetes, chronic back problems, allergies, obesity, and high blood pressure just to name a few.

4-5. How does your age and your present stage of life affect your loss, and in what ways? How do you feel you would be affected if the same loss happened to you when you were in earlier stages of your life? How about as you age, in future stages?

4-6. Explain to yourself the way in which cooperation can assist you in dealing with your loss. Cooperation is a two-way street. Look for ways you can give, so that you will better be able to accept help.

4-7. What questions do people ask you regarding your loss? Which of the questions are negative or uncomfortable for you? How have you handled matters when someone made you feel bad? And how have you handled a situation when the other person isn't asking the questions you feel they want to because he/she feels too embarrassed or sensitive to?

4-9. Have you discovered any myths or untrue beliefs about your type of loss or disability as a result of your personal experiences?

5 | Transforming Circumstance

Life comes at us in different ways—what makes the difference is not what happens to us but how we react to it. The Talmud says, "We see not what there is, but what we are." In this chapter, you will look closely at the circumstance of your loss.

For example, Janelle has had a mastectomy, and she is devastated. She feels that her identity as a female has been damaged, that she is no longer attractive, that her very reason for existence has been destroyed. In contrast, Sue underwent a double mastectomy as an elective procedure, in the belief that this will protect her from cancer she considers to have a high probability of affecting her. Once she has recovered from the operation, she is pleased with her inner feelings of improved safety, and she suffers no untoward psychological effects.

The physical loss is similar in the two cases. The two women think about the issue differently, and this affects everything about the way they react.

Miriam was dying of terminal cancer. All her life, she'd been busy—a doer, a helper, always there for others to the detriment of her own interests, not that she had acted the martyr. People felt comfortable in her company, and she'd always drop whatever she was doing to lend an ear, or a shoulder to cry on. But she rarely had time for herself. Now, she could do no more for anyone else, and for the first time since infancy, found herself on the receiving end. And, for the first time, she had leisure to think about deeper issues, the good and bad things in her past. And, despite her pain that the morphine couldn't quite control, and the restriction of her life to one room, and the loss of all her many previous concerns, Miriam found herself serene. She accepted her illness and coming death, and actually felt thankful that she was given this opportunity to take stock and find peace within her being.

Pete had been hit by a car as he walked alongside the road as a young adult. As a result, he had undergone about 35 to 40 surgeries the last time I spoke with him. These surgeries and recovery created many struggles for him and tested him right to the core of who he was, especially as a man. Pete has triumphed over so very many obstacles and come through to be a survivor. He accomplished this through therapy and Alcoholics Anonymous meetings and even went through a divorce in order to be able to live in health and safety.

In 1995, I rode with disabled cyclists from around the world in a brutal marathon challenge across more than 1,000 miles of Mongolia. I vividly recall two blind men who were particularly bold fellows; they rode on the back seats of a tandem providing power (stoking) to the bike as a sighted cyclist steered and braked the bike across very rough conditions. The trust that it took for these men to put their personal safety in the hands of thirty others whom they didn't know well in the beginning amazes me still. Eventually, they came to consider everyone to be brothers and sisters as the ride progressed across the world. They were definitely out of their element, especially in regard to finding their way to and from many venues of daily life. At times, they were upset that they needed help to find the latrine in the Gobi Desert, but in the end we all worked together and survived through teamwork.

5-1. Have you identified any positive events or factors related to your loss? These reactions need not be as powerful as for Miriam, even small positives are well worth identifying.

5-2. Using your family members and your friends or acquaintances, create an ideal family on paper. Make it the strongest possible support network for yourself that would help you cope most effectively with this loss.

5-3. Create a ritual that represents and memorializes your loss. For example, Rena was left with a permanent limp when her ex-husband broke into her house, shot her in the hip, then committed suicide by shooting himself in the head. For years she struggled with nightmares, guilt, the endless thoughts of 'what if'. Every time she walked, the limp and the stabs of pain she suffered were constant reminders of the trauma. She could never forget it, for her hip bore the scars. Finally, after considerable therapy and working on herself, she performed a ritual. She wrote a long letter to the man, and then asked all her family and friends around. In front of them all, she ceremonially burnt the letter, and his one remaining photograph. This didn't allow her to walk without a limp, but the physical handicap was no longer accompanied by the emotional one.

As another example, plant a tree or shrub demarcating a turning point—I can see it grow as I heal.[1]

Consider returning to a rehab center or back to the roots of the loss and remembering how far we have come. Give encouragement to others. One way of 'turning bad into good' is to become a support person for new sufferers of your type of loss.

---

[1] See also Rachel Pollack in The Power of Ritual (New York, Dell Publishing, 2000)

5-4. The Chinese language uses the same symbol in written form for 'crisis' and 'opportunity'. Has your experience of loss been both of these in any way? In what ways has your loss been a new start? An example is Don, who worked as a nurse, but after many years, hated it. He continued working simply because that was the easiest way to earn money. On one dark evening, he slipped on wet ground and tore a ligament in his shoulder. This meant that he could never work as a nurse again. Within a year, he had built a new profession for himself, one he would not have attempted if he had stayed stuck in the same rut.

5-6. Describe in detail how your loss occurred. Many people say that other people just don't understand. However, it is our responsibility to do our very best to describe our losses and explain how it has affected us so that others have an opportunity to understand. Often, it is only their understanding that allows assistance to be possible. For Carlie, such a description proved to give meaning to her life. She had been a heroin addict. She went 'cold turkey' in an attempt to give it up, and ended up in the hospital. She felt so terrible that she kept repeating, "I am going to kill myself!" The staff ignored her, and she jumped out the window. She broke her spine, and ended up as a paraplegic, at only twenty-four years of age. For a long time, she did her best to avoid remembering the details of her injury, trying to cope by denial. Finally, after a lot of work with a therapist, she was able to stand up to her memories. She then organized a program of visits to high schools, where she sat in her wheelchair, passionately telling her story to the students. She did a lot of good, warning them against the dangers of hard drugs.

5-7. What elements or factors allow you to feel more in control of your life?

5-8. What help are you able to ask for in satisfying your personal needs? And whom could you ask?

5-9 How visible is your loss and how does the visibility of it, or the lack of visibility, affect how you deal with it?

Graham had suffered a closed head injury, which resulted in significant short-term memory loss. He seemed normal to strangers, but was in fact severely handicapped. He coped by having his doctor write a short summary of his problem in everyday language. When Graham met new people, he smilingly handed them a copy. He used a notebook to write down every little snippet of information, and as long as others gave him the time, he could use this to carry on with most aspects of his life.

Sue had a different problem: a car accident involved disfiguring burns and scarring to her face. Repeated cosmetic surgery improved her appearance a great deal, but her face still drew the attention at first sight of many people. At first, she was intensely conscious of this and avoided contact, but eventually used humor as a weapon. She made up a six inch by four inch badge to wear. Written on it was, "You should have seen me before they fixed up my face!" This got a positive reaction from almost everyone.

6 The Ongoing Process of Loss and Recovery

"I refuse to allow a disability to determine how I live my life. I don't mean to be reckless, but setting a goal that seems a bit daunting actually is very helpful toward recovery."

—Christopher Reeve (1952-2004)

Christopher Reeve broke his neck in an equestrian competition in 1995. After a period of recovery involving physical therapy, he vowed never to give up. He then went on to star in four more films and directed two others after becoming a quadriplegic. Before his accident, his film career had been steady but tending toward smaller films. Afterward, he became an international symbol in his struggle for mobility and advocacy for the disabled. His foundation has distributed more than $60 million to both researchers and to non-profits that directly support quadriplegics. You can read his story of recovery and lessons for living in his book *Nothing Is Impossible*.

"When one's expectations are reduced to zero, one really appreciates everything one does have."

—Stephen Hawking (1942-)

Stephen Hawking was diagnosed with ALS[1] ("Lou Gehrig's Disease") at age 21 while still a college student. At the time, doctors gave him two or three more years to live as the best possible outcome. He was quite soon confined to a wheelchair but continued to pursue his study of mathematics and physics. He has remained an irresistible force in science despite progressive debilitation leading to paralysis and losing his voice. Hawking is most famous for his mathematical proof of the big-bang theory of the origin of the universe and work on related theories of black holes. Although a prodigious scientist, author, TV star, and winner of medals in astronomy and physics, he is still quite a down-to-earth family man and values his relationships most of all.

"The world will only give you what you ask for, nothing more, nothing less. Be very sure about what you ask."

—Tony Christiansen

Ever since a horrific railway accident left him without legs at age 9, Tony Christiansen has always moved forward by creating challenges and success in many areas of life. He is a qualified lifeguard with over 33 rescues to his name, has earned his private airplane pilot license, became a second degree black belt in Tae Kwon Do, and developed himself as a motivational author and speaker. Tony and his wife Elaine have been married since 1980 and have three children. You can read his autobiography in the book *Race You to the Top*.

---

[1] Amyotrophic Lateral Sclerosis (ALS) is characterized by the progressive loss of voluntary muscle contraction due to the destruction of nerve cells in the brain and the spinal cord that are responsible for the stimulation of the voluntary muscles. While the initial symptoms are subtle, the disease causes progressive physical disability. Mental functioning and physical sensation are spared. (source: Wikipedia)

Once you have completed the work up to here, take the time to review it monthly to see if you have any changes to record with any of the questions or assignments. The following questions in this chapter can help you re-assess your situation on a regular basis:

6-1. What, if anything, have you lost in the last month?

What, if anything, have you gained?

6-2. In what way has your present situation changed because of the losses and gains of the past month?'

6-3. How have your expectations and plans of the future been modified by the losses and gains of the past month?

6-4. Who in your life is making it easier for you to deal with your loss?

6-5. Who in your life is making your loss more difficult for you to deal with currently? This would include family, medical staff, rehabilitation staff, friends, work, and social services staff.

6-6-1. Who are the people in your life currently who can and will accept your loss?

6-6-2. How do you communicate with them and how can you make your needs known to them?

6-6-3. How are you able to contribute to the needs of other people?

6-7. What has been the thing you value most about your loss? I have discovered over time that there is a very clear possibility that we can grow from traumatic events in our lives. The growth pieces in our lives may not become apparent quickly, but as you review the past few weeks or months can you identify positive outcomes or patterns or tendencies that portray things that you have come to value as a result of your loss?

I can honestly say that my physical losses have brought me face to face with myself in ways that would have never happened otherwise. I have met people and been places and in situations I would have never encountered because of my loss. I have gained insights that can't be found in a classroom or in a textbook and to this day are very difficult to put into words. I have had opportunities which otherwise would have been inaccessible to me. I have gained more than I have lost.

Where to go from here: It's Your Choice

Loss, limits, nothingness, loneliness, different, odd, freak, weird, "that's cute", "what is his problem?" deafening silence...

At one time or another, the above words float in me or are thrown at me.

"Hey what is wrong with you?" the words or the look say it equally loud.

"Come here honey, don't get in his way" (translated at times as: stay away from him he is different.)

Do I remain vulnerable to the barbs and arrows of judgment or do I wall it off —dig a moat—pull up the drawbridge and build my walls higher and thicker to protect myself from them and perhaps even more importantly to protect them from me? After all I might splatter them in an unsuspecting moment

Do I learn to be numb and unfeeling? Or do I scorch them as napalm scorches the earth and all living things and create a momentary vacuum where all is briefly silent and all seems calm —but it is only the eye of the storm that broods within.

Or do I risk it all and perform emotional surgery on myself without anesthetic and push myself onto a frontier that I have not ventured onto ever before or, perhaps, I contain the festering poison and simply build the container bigger and reinforce it more thoroughly.

For me it is important—even critical —to do the surgery and create a balanced flow toward a peaceful life that exists within all our grasp. I believe that with God it is all possible.

EPILOGUE

My hope is that this workbook has contributed to your recovery process in a positive way. I also hope that it has helped you to heal further from your loss. I thank my clients over the years and my friends and acquaintances for their contribution to the ideas that have gone into this workbook. It is a struggle to cope with losses but it is possible to cope better if you develop a strategy and stick with it. It won't make the loss disappear but it may allow you to develop a handle of sorts for living with it. The path to recovery from a loss is often filled with obstacles, but as you consistently work through things that occur, inner peace about that loss is possible. In fact, as some of the examples show, people can sometimes gain immensely through having suffered a loss.

Peace to you as you make this journey.

About the Author

Until I was in the Marine Corps (in 1969) and injured my knee on the obstacle course at Officer Candidate School (OCS) as an enlisted man, I had never had any particular injuries. I had never needed corrective surgery for anything except appendix and tonsils in my short lifetime. However, being operated on in a military hospital and then recuperating as a resident in a 55-bed ward with primarily medevac cases directly returning from Viet Nam was a bit of an adjustment. I was an inpatient there for about 5 months and was operated on several times. I also did my primary rehab there. Even though I didn't recognize it at the time, this period turned out to be the biggest turning point in my life. That first injury and series of operations led to 13 knee operations and subsequent rehabs, mostly on one leg, but eventually the other knee had to be operated on as well in 1991.

Due to the damage and pain levels that existed with the first knee, it was finally fused in 1977 and surgically stiff for 20 years. This helped in some ways and created problems in others. Eventually, this led in 1997 to surgically unfusing the joint and implanting a prosthetic knee. I worked on rehab for a year and a half, three times a week to get it to function reasonably well and in a stable condition. There have been other affiliated problems with the leg, such as permanent nerve damage caused by medical negligence at one point, circulation problems and the periodic breakdown of the skin in areas affected by poorer circulation.

Overall, it was one of the best things that has ever happened to me, since it kept me from being shipped out to Viet Nam (I was issued six different sets of orders). Eventually, of course, it led me to the helping professions and making a difference in the lives of those suffering with the effects of physical and mental trauma. It has allowed me to meet people all over the world who have become special friends. In the end this has encouraged me even more—for example, if I am having a tough day, I think back to the triple-amputee Mongolian fireman I met who outrode even able-bodied riders each and every day. He did this for several weeks over hundreds of miles and I never saw a frown or a scowl on his face.

It has also been a teaching laboratory for me to learn about so many things and so many people and the many ways we can all learn to grapple with and ultimately come to terms with seeming overwhelming odds in such a wide array of approaches.

There are certainly things I miss from a physical standpoint such as playing handball and running daily, but I have found ways to replace at least partially some of those activities that were a big part of my self-care in the earlier years of my life.

Among my accomplishments: becoming an organic gardener; landscaping my yards; handcycle touring and racing; participating in the AXA World Ride from Mongolia to Beijing and St. Louis to Washington, D.C.; racing at the World Wheelchair Games in England in 1996; earning an MSW in my mid-forties. I am also proud of being able to raise my children and being a positive influence in the lives of my grandchildren.

Appendix 	Other Resources for Coping with Physical Loss	

Therapeutic Techniques

I have used **Traumatic Incident Reduction** (TIR) with many persons with physical loss and disabilities. TIR can address incidents of injury or of long-term illness that have resulted in chronic stress or anxiety. I also use the Unblocking procedure of TIR to help them resolve communication problems and have better relationships in their lives. For more information on TIR or to obtain a referral, please visit www.TIR.org.

I also use **EMDR**, a technique which has helped many to overcome the aftermath of their traumatic experiences. The EMDR Institute provides more information about Eye Movement Desensitization and Reprocessing (EMDR). See www.emdr.com

Last, I sometimes use **Emotional Freedom Therapy**, the technique commonly called 'tapping'. This has helped many find relief from anxiety and panic episodes, fears and phobias, and a wide variety of physical symptoms. A person can learn to use this technique themselves, and use its wide variety of applications to better assist themselves in overcoming many problems that hold them back from a better life. See www.emofree.com

Readings on Issues Related to Physical Loss and Disability

Anger

Thomas, S., and Jefferson, C. <u>Use Your Anger</u>. New York: Pocket Books, 1996.

Rich, Robert. <u>Anger and Anxiety: Be in charge of your emotions and control phobias</u>. Australia: Twilight Times Books, 2005. www.anxietyanddepression-help.com

Health

Topf. Linda. <u>You Are Not Your Illness</u>. New York: Fireside. 1995.

Reznik, Oleg, I. <u>The Secrets of Medical Decision Making: How to Avoid Becoming a Victim of the Health Care Machine</u>. Ann Arbor, MI: Loving Healing Press, 2006.

Inspiration

Bosco, Antoinette. <u>Finding Peace through Pain</u>. New York: Ballantine Books, 1995.

Chodron, Pema. <u>When Things Fall Apart</u>. Boston: Shambala Publications, 1997.

Mother Teresa. <u>In My Own Words</u>. New York: Random House. 1997.

Films on Issues Related to Physical Loss and Disability

Many of these films were originally in print as novels or biography. For more ideas, see www.disabilityfilms.co.uk and www.cinematherapy.com

Bone Collector, The (1999). Thriller/Mystery. Quadriplegic.

Born on the Fourth of July (1989). Biography/Drama/War. Paraplegic.

Brian's Song (1971). Biography/Drama/Sports. Cancer.

Coming Home (1978). Drama/War. Paraplegic.

Doctor, The (1991). Drama/Biography. Cancer.

Dying Young (1991). Drama/Romance. Cancer.

English Patient, The (1996). Drama/Romance/War. Burn victim.

Flight, The Theory Of (1998). Comedy/Drama/Romance. Motor neuron disease.

For Hope (1991). Drama. Scleroderma and lupus.

Forrest Gump (1994). Comedy/Drama. Mentally challenged.

Johnny Got His Gun (1971). Drama/War. Amputation, sensory loss.

Joan of Arcadia, Season 1 [Eps. 4, 5, 8, 12, 13, 21, and others] (2003). Paraplegic.

Joni (1980). Autobiography/Drama. Quadriplegic.

Love Affair, A: The Eleanor and Lou Gehrig Story (1978). ALS.

Mask (1985). Biography/Drama. Birth defect.

Million Dollar Baby (2004). Drama/Sports. Quadriplegic.

Murderball (2005). Documentary/Sports. Paraplegics and Paralympics.

My Left Foot (1989). Biography/Drama. Cerebral palsy.

Never Give Up: The Jimmy V Story (1996). Biography/Drama/Sports. Cancer.

On Golden Pond (1981). Drama/Comedy. Aging.

Other Side of the Mountain, The (1975). Biography/Drama. Quadriplegic.

Passion Fish (1992). Drama/Comedy. Paraplegic.

Ray (2004). Biography/Drama/Music. Sensory loss.

Rear Window (1998). Thriller/Mystery. Quadriplegic.

Ready, Willing, and Able (1999).

Sea Inside, The [El Mar Adentro] (2004). Biography/Drama. Quadriplegic.

Terms of Endearment (1983). Romance/Comedy. Cancer.

Terry Fox Story (1983). Biography/Drama/Sports. Cancer, amputee.

Through Riley's Eyes (2000). Short/Drama. ALS

Wit (2001). Drama. Cancer.

Guidelines for Watching Films

In preparation for each viewing session, sit comfortably. Let your attention move effortlessly, without strain, first to your body then to your breath. Simply inhale and exhale naturally. Follow your breath in this innocent, watchful way for a while. Notice any spots where there's tension or holding. As you grow aware of them, let your breath travel into these spots. To release tension you may experiment with "breathing into" any part of your body that feels strained. Never force your breath.

Your gentle attention is sufficient to help you become more present and balanced, as it spontaneously deepens and corrects your breathing if it is constricted. Experience your condition without inner criticizing or comment. If you notice yourself judging or narrating, simply listen to the tone of your inner dialog as you come back to your breath. Lay judgments and worries consciously aside.

As soon as you are calm and centered, start watching the movie. Most deeper insights arrive when you pay attention to the story and to yourself. While viewing, bring your inner attention to a holistic bodily awareness (felt sense). This means you are aware of "all of you" — head, heart, belly, etc. Once in a while you might notice your breathing from an inner vantage point — from your subtle, always-present intuitive core. Observe how the movie images, ideas, conversations and characters affect your breath. Don't analyze anything while you are watching. Be fully present with your experience.

Afterwards reflect on the following:

Do you remember whether your breathing changed throughout the movie? Could this be an indication that something threw you off balance? In all likelihood, what affects you in the film is similar to whatever unbalances you in your daily life.

Ask yourself: If a part of the film that moved you (positively or negatively) had been one of your dreams, how would you have understood the symbolism in it?

Notice what you liked and what you didn't like or even hated about the movie. Which characters or actions seemed especially attractive or unattractive to you? Did you identify with one or several characters?

Were there one or several characters in the movie that modeled behavior that you would like to emulate? Did they develop certain strengths or other capacities that you would like to develop as well?

Notice whether any aspect of the film was especially hard to watch. Could this be related to something that you might have repressed ("shadow")? Uncovering repressed aspects of our psyche can free up positive qualities and uncover our more whole and authentic self

Did you experience something that connected you to your inner wisdom or higher self as you watched the film?

It helps to write down your answers.

If some of the mentioned guidelines turn out to be useful, you might consider using them not only in "reel life" but also adapt them to "real life" because they are intended to make you become a better observer.

Excerpted with permission from www.CinemaTherapy.com by Birgit Wolz, PhD.

Suggested Reading for Coping with Physical Loss and Disability

Armstrong, Lance. It's Not About the Bike: My Journey Back To Life. New York: The Berkley Publishing Group, 2000.

Bennett, Michael. The Empathic Healer: An Endangered Species? San Diego, CA: Academic Press:, 2001.

Bluebond-Langer, Myra. In the Shadow of Illness: Parents and Siblings of the Chronically Ill Child. Princeton, NJ: Princeton University Press, 1996.

Brown, Christy. My Left Foot. London: Martin, Seeker & Warburg Limited, 1954.

Charlton, James. Nothing About Us Without Us: Disability, Oppression, and Empowerment. London: University of California Press, 1998.

Cleland, Max. Strong at the Broken Places: A Personal Story. Lincoln, VA: Chosen Books, 1980.

DeBecker, Gavin. Fear Less: Real Truth about Risk, Safety, and Security in a Time of Terrorism. New York: Little, Brown and Company, 2002.

Doka, Kenneth, Disenfranchised Grief: Recognizing Hidden Sorrow. New York: Lexington Books, 1989.

Ericsson, Stephanie. Companion Through the Darkness: Inner Dialogues on Grief. New York: Harper-Collins Publishers, 1993.

Ford, Michael. Wounded Prophet: A Portrait of Henri J.M. Nouwen. New York: Doubleday, 1999.

Hanh, Thich Nhat. Anger: Wisdom for Cooling the Flames. New York: Riverhead Books, 2001.

Hansel, Tim. You Gotta Keep Dancin'. Colorado Springs, CO: Cook Communications Ministries, 1985.

Hanson, Richard and Gerber, Kenneth. Coping with Chronic Pain: A Guide to Patient Self-Management. New York: The Guilford Press, 1990.

Hockenberry, John. Moving Violations: War Zones, Wheelchairs, and Declarations of Independence. New York: Hyperion, 1995.

Kovic, Ron. Born on the Fourth of July. New York: Akashic Books, 2005.

Kubler-Ross, Elisabeth. The Wheel of Life. A Memoir of Living and Dying. New York: Scribner, 1997.

Lewis, C.S. A Grief Observed. New York: HarperCollins Publishers, 1961.

Locke, Shirley. Coping with Loss: A Guide for Caregivers. Charles Springfield, IL: Thomas Pubs, 1994.

Markova, Dawna. I Will Not Die an Unlived Life: Reclaiming Purpose and Passion. Berkeley, CA: Conari Press, 2000.

Mercer, Dorothy. Injury: Learning to Live Again. Ventura, CA.: Pathfinder Publishing, 1994.

Millman, Dan. The Laws of Spirit: Simple, Powerful Truths of Making Life Work. Tiburon, CA: HJ Kramer Inc, 1995.

Millman, Dan. Sacred Journey of the Peaceful Warrior. Tiburon, CA: HJ Kramer Inc, 1991.

Myss, Caroline. Invisible Acts of Power: Personal Choices that Create Miracles. New York: Free Press, 2004.

Neeld, Elizabeth H. Seven Choices: Finding Daylight After Loss Shatters Your World. New York: Warner Books, 2003.

Nord, David. <u>Multiple AIDS-Related Loss: A Handbook for Understanding and Surviving a Perpetual Fall</u>. Washington, DC: Taylor & Francis, 1997.

Higgins, Gina O. <u>Resilient Adults: Overcoming a Cruel Past</u>. San Francisco: Jossey-Bass Inc. Publishers, 1994.

Pollack, Rachel. <u>The Power of Ritual</u>. New York: Dell Publishing, 2000.

Reeve, Jim. <u>God Never Wastes a Hurt</u>. Lake Mary, FL: Creation House, 2000.

Register, Cheri. <u>Living with Chronic Illness: Days of Patience and Passion</u>. New York: The Free Press, 1987.

Rich, Robert. <u>Cancer: A Personal Challenge</u>. Australian: Anina's Book Company, 2006. www.BobsWriting.com

Scaer, Robert C. <u>The Body Bears the Burden: Trauma, Dissociation. and Disease</u>. Binghamton, NY: The Haworth Medical Press, 2001.

Shapiro, Joseph. <u>No Pity: People with Disabilities Forging a New Civil Rights Movement</u>. New York: Times Books, 1993.

Siegel, Bernie. <u>Peace, Love and Healing: Body Mind Communication and the Path to Self-Healing: An Exploration</u>, New York: Harper & Row Publishers, 1989.

Taylor, Stacy. <u>Living Well with a Hidden Disability: Transcending Doubt and Shame and Reclaiming Your Life.</u> Oakland, CA: New Harbinger Publications, 1999.

Tada, Joni E. <u>Joni : An Unforgettable Story</u>. Grand Rapids, MI: Zondervan, 2001.

Traisman, Enid S. <u>I Remember, I Remember: A Keepsake Journal</u>. Omaha, NE: Centering Corp., 1992.

Volkman, M. <u>Life Skills: Improve the Quality of Your Life with Metapsychology</u>. Ann Arbor, MI: Loving Healing Press, 2005.

Volkman, V. <u>Beyond Trauma: Conversations on Traumatic Incident Reduction</u>. Ann Arbor, MI: Loving Healing Press, 2005

Wolz, Birgit. <u>E-Motion Picture Magic: A Movie Lover's Guide to Healing and Transformation</u>. New York: Glenbridge Publishing Ltd., 2004.

Yancey, Philip. <u>Disappointment with God: Three Questions No One Asks Aloud</u>. Grand Rapids, MI: Zondervan, 1988.

Yancey, Philip. <u>Where is God When it Hurts?</u> Grand Rapids, MI: Zondervan, 1990.

Periodicals

Paraplegic News. www.pvamagazines.com/pnnews/

Sports 'N Spokes Magazine. www.pvamagazines.com/sns

For Therapists Working with Physical Loss and Disability

Ader, Robert. Psychoneuro-immunology. Orlando, FL: Academic Press. 1991.

Clark, E., Fritz, J. and Rieker, P. Clinical Sociological Perspectives on Illness & Loss: The Linkage of Theory and Practice. Philadelphia: The Charles Press Publications, 1990.

Cooper, C. and Watson, M. Cancer and Stress: Psychological, Biological, and Coping Studies. New York: John Wiley & Sons, 1991.

Costa, Paul Jr. and VandenBos, G. Psychological Aspects of Serious Illness: Chronic Conditions, Fatal Diseases, and Clinical Care. Washington, DC: American Psychological Assoc, 1990.

Hertman, Sandra. Grief and the Healing Arts: Creativity as Therapy. Amityville, NY: Baywood Publishing Company, 1999.

Margoles, M. and Weiner, R. Chronic Pain: Assessment, Diagnosis, and Management. New York: CRC Press, 1999.

Marinelli, R. and Orto, A.D. The Psychological and Social Impact of Disability. New York: Springer, 1991.

Piper, W., McClallum, M. & Azim, H. Adaptation to Loss Through Short-Term Group Psychotherapy. New York: The Guilford Press, 1992.

Pollin, Irene. Medical Crisis Counseling: Short-Term Therapy for Long-Term Illness. New York: W.W. Norton & Company, Inc., 1995.

Rando, Therese. Treatment of Complicated Mourning. Champaign, IL: Research Press, 1993.

Shapiro, C.H. When Part of the Self is Lost: Helping Clients Heal after Sexual and Reproductive Losses. San Francisco: Jossey-Bass Inc.Publishers, 1993.

Appendix B

Organizations That Can Help

Support Foundations and Associations

American Academy of Allergy, Asthma, and Immunology
611 E. Wells St, Suite 1100
Milwaukee, WI 53202
1-800-822-2762; 414-272-6071
Website: www.aaaai.org
Email: info@aaaai.org

American Cancer Society
1599 Clifton Road NE
Atlanta, GA 30329
1-800-227-2345
Website: www.cancer.org

American Chronic Pain Association
P.O. Box 850, Rocklin, CA 95677
Tel: 916-632-0922;
Website: www.theacpa.org
Email: acpa@ix.netcom.com

ACPA exists to facilitate peer support and education for individuals with chronic pain and their families so that these individuals may live more fully in spite of their pain. They also work to raise awareness among the health care community, policy makers, and the public at large about issues of living with chronic pain.

American Diabetes Association
P.O. Box 25757, 1660 Duke Street
Alexandria, VA 22314
1-800-232-3472;
Website: www.diabetes.org

American Heart Association
7272 Greenville Avenue, Dallas, TX 75231
1-800-242-1793; 1-800-AHA-USA1
Website: www.americanheart.org
Email: inquire@americanheart.org

American Liver Foundation

1425 Pompton Avenue,
Cedar Grove, NJ 07009
1-800-223-0179; Tel: 201-256-2550
Fax: 973-256-3214
Website: www.liverfoundation.org
Email: info@liverfoundation.org

Arthritis Foundation
1330 West Peachtree Street
Atlanta, GA 30309

1-800-283-7800; Fax: 404-872-8694
Website: arthritis.org
Email: help@arthritis.org

Crohn's and Colitis Foundation
386 Park Avenue South
New York, NY 10016
1-800-932-2423 x 257; Tel: 212-685-3440
Fax: 212-779-4098
Website: WWW.ccfa.org
Email info@ccfa.org

Endometriosis Association International Headquarters
8585 N. 76111 Place, Milwaukee, WI 53223
1-800-992-3636; Tel: 414-355-2200; Fax: 414-355-6065
Website: www.endometriosisassn.org
Email: endo@endometriosisassn.org

Job Accommodation Network
PO Box 6080, Morgantown, WV 26506-6080
1-800-526-7234
Website: www.jan.wvu.edu
Email: jan@jan.wvu.edu

JAN is a free consulting service designed to increase the employability of people with disabilities by: providing individualized worksite accommodations solutions, providing technical assistance regarding the ADA and other disabil-

ity related legislation, and educating callers about
self-employment options.

Lupus Foundation of America
2000 L Street, N.W., Suite 710
Washington, DC 20036
1-800-558-0121; 202-349-1155
Fax: 202-349-1156
Website: www.lupus.org
Email: info@lupus.org

National Chronic Pain Outreach Association
7979 Old Georgetown Road, Suite 100
Bethesda, MD 20814
Tel: 301-652-4948;
Website: www.chronicpain.org;
Email mcp04@aol.com

NCPOA's purpose is to lessen the suffering of
people with chronic pain by educating pain sufferers, health care professionals, and the public
about chronic pain and its management. They
can put you in touch with a local support group.

National Headache Foundation
428 W. St. James Place, Chicago, IL 60614
1-800-843-2256; Fax: 773-525-7357
Website: www.headaches.org

National Multiple Sclerosis Society
733 Third Avenue, 6th Floor
New York, NY 10017-3288
1-800-344-4867; Tel: 212.986.3240
Fax: 212-986.7981
Website: www.nmss.org
Email: info@nmss.org

Paralyzed Veterans of America
Offers information, publications on a variety of
topics of interest to veterans and all people with
spinal-cord injury/disease.
801 Eighteenth Street NW
Washington, DC 20006
1-800-424-8200
Website: www.pva.org
Email: info@pva.org

Sickle Cell Disease Association of America
200 Corporate Pointe, Suite 495
Culver City, CA 90230
1-800-421-8453
Website: www.sicklecelldisease.org;

Sports Support Organizations

Amputee Sports

Disabled Sports USA
Web: www.dsusa.org
Phone 301-217-0960

DS/USA offers nationwide sports rehabilitation programs to anyone with a permanent disability. Activities include winter skiing, water sports, summer and winter competitions, fitness and special sports events. Participants include those with visual impairments, amputations, spinal cord injury, dwarfism, multiple sclerosis, head injury, cerebral palsy, and other neuromuscular and orthopedic conditions. As a member of the United States Olympic Committee, DS/USA sanctions and conducts competitions and training camps to prepare and select athletes to represent the United States at the Summer and Winter Paralympic Games.

Lakeshore Foundation
Web: www.lakeshore.org;
Email: susank@lakeshore.org
Phone: 205-313-7400

Lakeshore Foundation promotes independence for persons with physically disabling conditions and opportunities to pursue active healthy lifestyles. In February of 2003, the United States Olympic Committee (USOC) designated Lakeshore Foundation as the first-ever, official USOC Training Site for both Olympic and Paralympic sports.

National Amputee Golf Association
Web: www.nagagolf.org;
Email: b1naga@aol.com
Phone: 800-633-6242

NAGA currently has over 2,000 members in the U.S. and some 200 players from 17 other countries. In addition to its national tournament, NAGA hosts events for senior players and sponsors local and regional tournaments throughout the country. The Golf for the Physically Challenged program has enabled many to realize firsthand that they can play the game and have fun in an outdoor sport. NAGA brought its First Swing program to hospitals and rehabilitation centers throughout the U.S. in 1989.

Archery

Disabled Archery USA
Web: www.disabledArcheryUSA.org;
Email: disabledarcheryusa@comcast.net

Wheelchair Sports USA
See write-up on p. 88.

Basketball

Canadian Wheelchair Basketball Association
Web: www.cwba.ca;
Email: cwba@cwba.ca

International Wheelchair Basketball Association
Web: www.iwbf.org;
Email: morchard@mts.net

National Wheelchair Basketball Association
Web: www.nwba.org;
Email: kingbee@bellsouth.net

Billiards

National Wheelchair Poolplayer Association, Inc.
Web: www.nwpainc.org;
Email: charlie@nwpainc.org

Bowling

American Wheelchair Bowling Association
Web: www.awba.org;
Email: bowlawba@aol.com

Fencing

United States Fencing Association
Web: www.usfencing.org;
Email: info@usfencing.org
The USFA is the national governing body for wheelchair fencing

Flight

Freedom's Wings International
Web: www.freedomswings.org
Email: murph771@bellatlantic.net

International Wheelchair Aviators
Web: www.wheelchairaviators.org
Email: IWAviators@aol.com

Football
Universal Wheelchair Football Association
http://dept.kent.edu/stuorg/AUWorld/UWF.html
Email: John.Kraimer@UC.Edu

Golf
US Golf Association
Web: www.usga.org
http://www.usga.org/playing/rules/golfers_with_disabilities.html
The USGA is the national governing body for wheelchair golfing

National Amputee Golf Association
See write-up on p. 87.

Handcycling
US Handcyling Federation
Web: www.ushf.org
Email: info@ushf.org

Getting together with a bunch of other riders and going out for a group ride is a great way to learn more about the sport, find new rides to go on and learn more about the wonderful art of drafting.

Hockey
Canadian Electric Wheelchair Hockey Association
Web: www.geocities.com/cewha/
Email: daube@whitecapcanada.com

US Sled Hockey Assocation
Web: www.sledhockey.org
Email:craig@sledhockey.org

Sled hockey is the fast, exciting, rumble-tumble version of ice hockey played primarily by people with mobility disabilities. The game is essentially the same as any "stand-up" ice hockey game with the major difference being that all of the players sit in a sled which is attached to two hockey skate blades under the seat.

Horseback Riding
North American Riding for the Handicapped Association
Web: www.narha.org
Email: NARHA@NARHA.ORG

NARHA promotes the benefit of the horse for individuals with physical, emotional and learning disabilities. For individuals with disabilities, equine-assisted activities have been shown to improve muscle tone, balance, posture, coordination, motor development as well as emotional well-being.

National Disability Sports Alliance
Web: www.ndsaonline.org
Email: diavolio@ndsaonline.org

The competition is in dressage. The majority of physical disabilities are eligible. Equestrian has its own functional classification system. There are four grades for riders based on how they function.

Backcountry Discovery
Web: www.backcountrydiscovery.org
Email: mailto:bcd@frii.com

Multi-Sport
Adaptive Adventures
Web: www.adaptiveadventures.org
Email: info@ushf.org

Casa Colina Adaptive Sports and Outdoor Adventures
Web: www.casacolina.org
Email: rehab@casacolina.org

Examples of this program's activities include camping, dog-sledding, cycling, fishing, whale watching, horse-pack trips, jet skiing, snow skiing, and white water rafting.

Disabled Sports USA
See writeup on p. 87

Wheelchair Sports USA
Web: www.wsusa.org
Email: wsusa@aol.com

An organization dedicated to facilitating competitive sporting events including archery, track, shooting, swimming, table tennis, and weightlifting.

World T.E.A.M. Sports
Web: www.worldteamsports.org
Email: info@worldteamsports.org

Quad Sports

Bay Area Outreach & Recreation Program
Web: www.borp.org
Email: borp@borp.org
BORP offers a number of competitive sports programs, as well as outdoor adventures, family outings, and integrated cycling in the SF Bay area.

US Quad Rugby Association
Web: www.quadrugby.com
Email: usqra@quadrugby.com

Shooting

PVA National Trapshoot Circuit
Web: www.pva.org
Email: wpva@biggamehuntinggear.com or GeoffH@pva.org
Hosted by Paralyzed Veterans of America chapters across the USA for men and women who are beginners, novices, veterans, civilians, wheelchair users, or able-bodied shooters.

Skiing

Disabled Sports USA
See writeup on p. 87

Ski For All Foundation
Web: www.skiforall.org
Email: info@skiforall.org

Ski For Light (Alpine)
Web: www.sfl.org
Email: info@sfl.org

Tennis

International Tennis Federation (Wheelchair Dept.)
Web: www.itftennis.com
Email: wheelchairtennis@ itftennis.com

US Tennis Association
Web: www.usta.com, click on *USA Wheelchair Tennis*

Water Sports & Recreation

Abili-Ski Adaptive Watersports
Web: www.abili-ski.com
Email: chris@abili-ski.com

Access To Sailing
Web: www.accesstosailing.org
Email: info@accesstosailing.org

Adaptive Aquatics
Web: www.adaptiveaquatics.org
Email: info@adaptiveaquatics.org

Anchors Away, Dept of Neurology
Contact Dave Sewell, sewelldh@musc.edu
843-7920721

Disabled Sailing Holidays
Web: www.disabledsailingholidays.com
Email: dryachting@hotmail.com

Handicapped Scuba Association
Web: www.hsascuba.com
Email: hsa@hsascuba.com

U CanSki 2
http://ucanski2.tripod.com/1.html
Email: Annsitski@aol.com

US Rowing Association
Web: www.usrowing.org
Email: members@usrowing.org

USA Waterski
Web: usawaterski.org

Wheelchair Sports USA / Swimming
Web: www.wsusa.org, click on *Disabled*
Email: wsusa@aol.com

Weightlifting

US Wheelchair Weightlifting Foundation
Phone: 215-945-1964

INDEX

Beyond Trauma:
Conversations on Traumatic Incident Reduction, 2nd Ed.

Victor Volkman (Ed.) takes the mystery out of one of the more remarkably effective clinical procedures in a way that can help millions of people revitalize and improve their lives. To those desperate people who have experienced trauma or tragedy, this process is a pathway to dealing with their feelings and getting on with their lives

In the new book **Beyond Trauma: Conversations on Traumatic Incident Reduction**, Volkman presents a series of conversations with a wide range of people from many different backgrounds and experiences. Each provides his or her perspective on Traumatic Incident Reduction, or TIR for short. The book explains the techniques used by professionals and patients to help people sort out, resolve and overcome the negative effects of painful suffering.

Readers will learn about how TIR has helped domestic violence survivors, crime victims, Vietnam vets, children, and others.

"Not in 30+ years of practice have I used a more remarkably effective clinical procedure."
—Robert Moore, PhD

Praise *for Beyond Trauma*

"*Beyond Trauma* outlines the elements with clarity and insight as to how TIR will resolve wrestling with dilemmas, understanding your demons, and climbing out of emptiness."
—Sherry Russell, Grief Management Specialist and Author

"Our staff therapist is finding Beyond Trauma very helpful".
—Joan M. Renner, Director, Sexual Assault Program, YWCA of Clark County, WA

"*Beyond Trauma* is a recommended book for the professional or for the lay reader who wants to know about this technique before possibly seeking out a practitioner.
—Harold McFarland, Readers Preference Reviews

"*Beyond Trauma: Conversations on Traumatic Incident Reduction* is an excellent resource to begin one's mastery in this area of practice."
—Michael G. Tancyus, LCSW, DCSW, Augusta Behavioral Health

"*Beyond Trauma* is a very well organized and persuasive combination of viewpoints, of a sort too seldom found in single volumes describing therapeutic tools."
—Review by Gerald French, author of *Traumatic Incident Reduction*

"*Beyond Trauma* is a welcome and much appreciated contribution to professional and academic reference collections and supplemental reading lists."
—Midwest Book Review, Editor's Choice Award

"TIR is meant as a complete resolution of the issue behind these traumatic events rather than a coping mechanism or a cathartic episode. Rating 8/10."
—Tami Brady, Blether.com Reviews

Loving Healing Press
5145 Pontiac Trail
Ann Arbor, MI 48105

(734)662-6864

info@LovingHealing.com
Distributed by Baker & Taylor, Ingram, Quality Books, and New Leaf Distributing.

Pub. March 2005 — 360 pp trade/paper — 7"x9"
ISBN-13 978-1-932690-04-0— $22.95 Retail

Includes appendices, biblio., resources, and index.
For general and academic libraries.

http:/www.BeyondTrauma.com

Exclusive offer for readers of *Coping with Physical Loss: A Workbook*

Share Loving Healing Press Books with a colleague, friend, or loved one.
Order direct from the publisher with this form and save!

Order Form – 15% Discount Off List Price!

Ship To:

_____

Name

_____

Address

_____

Address

_____

City   **State**

_____

District   **Country**   **Zip/Post code**

_____

Daytime phone #   **email address**

☐ VISA   ☐ MasterCard   ☐ US$ check paid to

Loving Healing Press

_____   _____/_____

Card #   **Expires**

_____

Signature

Coping with Physical Loss...   _____ x $14.50 = _____

Beyond Trauma: Conversations... _____ x $20.00 = _____

Life Skills: Improve the Quality...   _____ x $14.50 = _____

Residents of Michigan: please add 6% tax _____

Postage & Handling (see below) $_____

Your Total _$_____

Shipping price _per copy_ via:
☐ Priority Mail (+ $3.50)   ☐ Int'l Surface (+ $5)   ☐ USA MediaMail/4th Class (+ $2)

Fax Order Form back to (734)663-6861 or
Mail to LHP, 5145 Pontiac Trail, Ann Arbor, MI 48105

Printed in the United States
71130LV00002B